Iron
Mountain

Also
by
Mark
Frutkin

Poetry

Fiction

Iron Mountain

poems by

Mark Frutkin

Porcepic Books
an imprint of

Beach Holme Publishing
Vancouver

To my good friend, Henry Chapin

This book is published by Beach Holme Publishing, 226–2040 West 12th Avenue, Vancouver, B.C. V6J 2G2. *www.beachholme.bc.ca*. This is a Porcepic Book.

The publisher gratefully acknowledges the financial support of the Canada Council for the Arts and of the British Columbia Arts Council. The publisher also acknowledges the financial assistance received from the Government of Canada through the Book Publishing Industry Development Program (BPIDP) for its publishing activities.

The Canada Council | Le Conseil des Arts
for the Arts | du Canada

BRITISH
COLUMBIA
ARTS COUNCIL
Supported by the Province of British Columbia

Editor: Michael Carroll
Production and Design: Jen Hamilton
Cover Art: *Landscape* by Wu Jingting, from the exhibition *Masterpieces of 20th Century Chinese Painting* organized by the **Canadian Foundation for the Preservation of Chinese Cultural and Historical Treasures** and the **China International Exhibition Agency**.
Author Photograph: Sandra Russell

Printed and bound in Canada by Houghton Boston, Saskatoon.

National Library of Canada Cataloguing in Publication Data

Frutkin, Mark, 1948-
  Iron mountain

  "A Porcepic book."
  ISBN 0-88878-424-4

  I. Title.
PS8561.R84I76 2001   C811'.54   C2001-911072-3
PR9199.3.F776I76 2001

Contents

Acknowledgements

Some of the poems in this book were previously published (in several cases in slightly altered form) in the following anthologies and publications:

Descant: "Prisoner," "First Snow of Silence," "Crackle-Glaze"

The Fiddlehead: "Wall"

The Free Verse Anthology: "Report on the End of Time"

Indian Literature (India): "Early Winter Light"

Intervox: "Deep Ecology Haiku"

Poetry Canada Review: "Baudelaire's Letter to Ancelle," "Double," "Degas in New Orleans," "Creation Myths"

Prism international: "Villa-Lobos Lugs His Cello Through the Amazon Jungle"

Revista Española de Estudios Canadienses: "Thunder"

Sealed in Struggle (anthology edited by N. Vulpe and M. Albari): "Death of a Poet"

Six Ottawa Poets (anthology edited by S. Mayne): "Chinese Exhibition," "Cigar Box," "Lombardy Poplars," "Old Bones," "On Reading Submissions to a Poetry Magazine," "Reinventing the World"

White Wall Review: "Tintoretto"

The Windhorse Review: "Fragments of Heaven and Earth," "Euclid," "Blue Sky," "Horses in the Fetal Heart Rate," "Once a Great Ruler, This Spider," "Heart of Rust"

Within the size of a fist can be assembled the beauty of a thousand cliffs.... The Sage (Confucius) once said, "the humane man loves mountains." ... Thus longevity through quietude is achieved through this love.

—Kong Chuan,
preface to *Hermit of Cloudy Forest* by Du Wan, 1133

Book I

Iron Mountain

The
Journey
to
Shu
—A
Chinese
Landscape

1. A Horsehair Brush

The artist paints with a brush of horsehair
drawn from the horse he is painting.

Mountains and forests, ambiguous,
their folds spontaneous and immeasurable.
Ambiguous too the path
threading through them
like smoke
rising from a mountain hut.
At first it holds steady,
a solid stream,
then splays and shreds
in a thousand branches.

Why are we going to Shu? Remind me,
the Emperor on his majestic horse
questions his lieutenant.

To see the goddess, the lieutenant replies.
The Emperor turns his head, shakes
the reins, and the single-file procession
stutters on through birch forests.

One day the weather is clear, the next, cloudy.
As the painting unfolds, so do the mountains,
so does the path through the mountains,
and so does the line of men and horses
on the path through the mountains.

Not even the painter knows
why they are going to Shu.

2. The Emperor Comes to the Wall

Deep in the chaos of mountains
the Emperor and his procession
come to a wall.
Like a snake
or a flickering tail
of lightning,
the wall twists along
mountain ridges
until it disappears to the east
until it disappears to the west.

The peasants they ask do not know
how far the wall goes
but believe it must end
two mountain chains beyond.
But they have never walked that far,
east *or* west.

The Emperor and his procession
follow the wall toward the setting sun
until they can ride no farther
and turn about.
On arriving at their starting point
they rest, then ride again
toward the rising sun
until they can ride no farther
and turn about.

When they have returned once again
to their starting point,
the Emperor is haunted
by the belief that
if he had kept on one day more

in either direction
he would have come to the wall's end.

His lieutenant watches him rise
in his stirrups to gaze eastward,
then turn to the west.
His horse twists in a circle
unsure which way to go.
The Emperor sighs and waits
and does nothing.
The long procession of riders and horses
waits too, in silence.
He is waiting for a message from heaven.
The dusk descends and still they wait.
The wall twists and untwists
through knotted skeins of mountains.
No one moves.
Night comes.

3. The Emperor's Poem

The iron mountain towers above us
robed in mist, its crags
reach through the clouds into heaven,
a single white waterfall seems
to thread down from the sky
in steps and fragments
and, like the trail behind us,
disappears the way we have come.

I see my lieutenant ahead
alone on his horse.
He reminds me of myself.
Though I am the greatest Emperor
the world has ever known,
the mountain towering above
was here before I came,
will remain when I have gone.

The first heavy rain will obliterate
our footprints and any sign of our passing.
In ten springs, a hundred, a thousand,
this path will remain the signature
of a traveller unknown, and the mist
will continue to swirl and dissipate
like poems breathed on air.

4. Chaos

Like the mountains that sweep before us,
fragmented and overlapping,
our world is in chaos.
My failure to bring order to my world
stings me and causes me distress.
I am the Emperor,
yet the world is an avalanche of sorrows
and I can do nothing.

Long ago I gave up searching
yet I ride on.

I take my ease in a poor man's hut.
How is it my heart is soothed
by the sight of two wooden buckets
resting side by side in the doorway?

5. The Emperor Comes to the River

I have come through a storm
of mountains to find Guan Yin,*
high peaks and low valleys,
my heart torn and contorted
as the concatenation of cliffs,
the constant rupture of planes.

All the streams have dissolved in the river,
twisted down from the mountains
and dissolved in the river.
The water flows without obstruction
like thoughts with no one attached to them.

*Goddess of Compassion

Mountains, Clouds

Meditation on a Mountain

It begins and ends with a mountain.
A waterfall chatters down its face
turns to a whispering brook
widens, flattens into a slow river
resolves into a calm lake
where the mountain melts
in its pure reflection.

Mountain and Cloud

Mountains so high
it is impossible to distinguish
what is mountain, what is cloud.

In the pavilion
at the mountain's foot,
a lute
wrapped in brocade
woven to the sound
of the lute's music,
depicting a scene
of mountains and cloud,
and a lute in a pavilion,
wrapped in brocade.

Wang Meng's Painting "Reading in Spring Mountains"

A circular stamp above the mountains,
the Chinese character for moonlight.
Cursive tree branches tell stories
of prevailing winds, dry summers, long deep winters.
The creases of the mountains
cut tales deep into the memory of the earth.
Clouds brush themselves into wavering ideograms,
and dissolve like secret writing hidden in the skies.

A Poem Written on "Hall of Clear Mind" Paper

Paper is the most humble of the Four Treasures: paper, brush, ink, inkstone.

Slight breeze across the page.
Not much to say.
No mountain. No storm.
Cherish the earth.
Cherish the paper,
the trees this is written in
as wind, invisible ink,
weaves among branches.
Nothing much happens.
Only the effect is visible.

The Emperor Floats

for Richard Gravel

The Emperor sits on his throne
at the centre of his palace.
Retinues of servants and messengers
come and go with unrelieved persistence,
but he is alone, always alone.
He has come through the mountains,
layers of mountains,
mountains of time and earth,
of light and shadow,
of wind and dust.

The Emperor no longer falls through space
like a comet with its hair on fire.
He floats now, 1/78th of an inch above his throne.
He is still in the world
but the world is no longer in him,
mountains have turned to clouds
the vastness of space becomes the sound of a bell
rung once on a cool sunlit morning.

Disappearance

The chorus of birds at dawn tells him it is spring.
Among sheer mountains and tangled streams
he walks with staff in hand,
barely legible among mists, clouds, and crags,
a bit of calligraphy come to life.

He walks on and on deeper still
into farther reaches of mountain ridges
and never comes to the final peak.
The mountains go on forever, inside and out.
He never solves their riddle
never penetrates their ambiguity.
He wanders deeper, back into the heart of the earth,
days turn into weeks, weeks into months, months into years.
Sometimes the path rises, sometimes it descends,
in harmony with the stream that accompanies his travels.
Springs turn to summer, red leaves and falling needles
give way to a landscape glowing with snow.
He has lost all desire to reach the highest peak,
content that the mountains go on and on
without end, as the stream beside him
never ceases its gurgling
like an infant learning to speak.

Brushstroke

No stars behind the clouds.
How could something as vast as a mountain,
there moments before, disappear?
Trees and rocks vanish.
No moon.
Silent wanderer swallowed by darkness.
I can hardly believe I exist.
I don't. I'm gone
but for a faint glow of thoughts,
phosphorescence dissolving
into night's exquisite ink.

High above the ridge, suddenly
clouds part—
brushstroke of light.

Inside Gatineau Park

The ancient Chinese believed
streams symbolized mind
while the mountain was the heart.

I walk deep into Gatineau Park
along a trail little travelled
by noisy hikers or mountain bikes.
I sit on an outcrop of rock
beside a tranquil pond.
The slight hump of stone
under me is iron mountain,
wherever you sit, wherever
you find yourself,
the earth a good mother
with a strong and open heart,
the earth a good mother
who helped you to walk,
to rise for a while and be human,
and then takes you back
takes you back again
where you can be what you were
before you were born.

Chinese
Shards

Chinese Exhibition

A carillon of six bronze bells,
mutes with nightingale dreams
from the Age of Autumns and Springs,
tongue-tied with time.

Two terra-cotta musicians stand,
their long thin bodies like musical reeds
hands placed just so, but empty,
their instruments turned to constellations,
following a music unheard by us.

Inside the museum case
a jar of clear water,
three thousand years evaporating
into nothing, leaving
a subtle calligraphy of minerals
on the jar's glass bottom.

A Taoist priest gulps the elixir
of immortality and blows away
in the dust,
a young Chinese girl
bumps me in the crowd
prompting a shiver
like a startled phoenix
dressed in my skin.

Seven Buddhas

Wood Buddha.
With time and damp it split and cracked
and new stems sent forth green leaves.

Bronze Buddha.
Wind-driven sand
scoured its shine into dull armour.

Stucco Buddha.
First the paint, then the fine stucco,
then the coarse stucco fell to earth
leaving a skeleton of wood.

Stone Buddha.
Worn back into a piece of the mountain.

Paper Buddha.
Folds caught light, words faded.

Snow Buddha.
Now the river, now the sea.

Ice Buddha.
Could see through to its heart,
nothing there.

Fragments of Heaven and Earth

In the Royal Ontario Museum
I learn the peoples north of China's borders
were fond of drinking fermented mare's milk.
Later, a pot of hot saki with lunch
at a sushi restaurant.

The *xieze*, imaginary beast with overlapping
scales down its chest, paws, and a flaming aura,
could distinguish between good and evil.

Du Wan on stone (1133): "Within the size of a fist
can be assembled the beauty of a thousand cliffs."
And Confucius: "The humane man loves mountains,"
not to mention words that almost, not quite, rhyme.
For the Chinese, the mountain symbolizes the heart,
the humane man sees a dignified peace reflected there,
another kind of, almost, not quite, rhyme.

Zhou Qutei on navigation (1178): "Ships…
traverse several tens of thousands of *li* with hundreds
of human lives dependent on a single rudder."
This morning's *Globe and Mail* headline told of sudden increases
in the price of oil from a single supertanker spill
off the coast of Alaska.

Objects: A Song Dynasty mirror of bronze no longer
reflects, now "dulled or green from corrosion in burial."
A porcelain water pot for holding a scholar's ink,
a subtle design, dragon and phoenix entwined.

"Ideally, the library (of the scholar) had a window
looking into a tranquil yet inspiring view."
The view from this desk in room 321 at the Park Plaza:
a corner of Avenue Road, a side street, several trees

without leaves, grey March light, traffic, sirens.
"Tranquil yet inspiring" is a state of mind,
an ancient Chinese garden cloistered behind the eyes,
an immortal space that allows mountain, bird song, truck engine.

In the Bishop White Gallery at the ROM, among
the unmoving, eternally vigilant eyes of the bodhisattvas,
a handful of awkward dancers stroke at tai chi.

After viewing a huge statue of Buddha Vairocana,
I glimpse a thousand Buddhas in a distorted sheet
                              of native copper.

In the museum washroom, five white Crane urinals
in a row glow like pure Chinese porcelain vessels.

The Scholar Breathes a Sigh of Relief on Failing the Civil Service Exam for the Third Time

for Murray Wilson

I never wanted to spend my precious days
trapped in intrigues at the capital,
its twisted narrow alleys a nest of plots.
I never desired to become a mandarin or merchant
amassing mountains of wealth
to be frittered away by foolish descendants,
the paper bills food for worms,
coins melted down into arms and helmets.
I merely longed to spend quiet days
gazing out a brilliant southern window
over a garden courtyard,
a bit of a hermit deep in conversation
with the ancients with whom I had more in common
than the ghosts who walked my streets.
My books are piled high—I will even
reread some if I so desire,
and share the occasional pot of wine
with a friend who speaks my language.

Silkworm

Nothing in the world
tastes like mulberry leaves.
And I cling to this unshakable
memory of wings.
You never had wings,
the others inform me, *never.*
I don't know.
I do know this:
one day we'll die a horrible death.
Nobody says "die a wonderful death."
The heat will grow unbearable,
our fluids will dry up.

But I know a few of us
will be removed, taken
from this place
and allowed to unfold.

I remember the opalescent sky
above the trees,
Oh, how I love
the taste of mulberry.
I never tire of it,
or of moving my head
in a figure eight,
the silk spewing from my mouth
as I wrap myself
in my own shroud.

How do they choose the ones
allowed to unfold?
Or do we somehow choose ourselves?
Do those with the strongest

memory of wings
imagine them again?

The others will be unravelled,
appear later in a fine
lady's yellow silk dress,
though they won't remember.

Book II

Wilderness

Measuring
Dust

A Drunk Addresses the Night Sky

Argues with stars,
questions their logic, their patterns,
why this order and no other?
Confers concerning distant light geometries.
The stars listen.
No need to shout into vast silence,
whisper to the ends of the universe,
word travels,
speed of thought.
Is he dizzy? Does he stumble?
Do they, the stars, shivering with cold?
What is the logic of this place?
Silence.

Measuring Dust

We humans never quite fit,
magnetic north versus true north,
mean time versus solar time,
our machines never quite measure up,
our clocks can always find
time more precise,
the only sure proof of imprecision.
We never quite figure it out,
the stars a chaos of intersecting
grids, overlapping domes
we have imagined, all of it.
We have imagined all of it.
Measuring dust.

Space

How do you hatch a bowl of worms
into a sky full of monarchs
or a night thick with moths?
The great tree dances before me—
could be a witch, could be my lover.
A little of both?
I'm falling in, falling inside.
The light is flagrant,
darkness raw and exotic,
both there where it's totally empty.
So empty anything could happen next,
anything—a bird chirps, distant
acceleration of traffic, a fly
tours my office.
But I'm falling inside
as if the cave of my heart
were vast space, maybe my organs
are distant planets separated
from each other by the space
between the flag stilled
and the flag waving,
as a red-and-white rectangle of cloth
fixed to a white pole
responds to clear wind
and then doesn't.

Euclid

His name is Euclid and he's drowning
in torn bits of newspaper,
up to his eyeballs in shredded books,
random half-lines, broken words, pages disassembling.
Someone keeps turning the radio on and off
like the sea breaking at the edge
like the sea breaking into tears
and mumbling incoherent raptures,
foam at the corners of its mouth.
Euclid is flying apart—his *t*'s left uncrossed,
his *i*'s undotted.
He's hanging upside down in Magellan's sea,
triangles, circles, squares fall from his pockets,
a rain of light on our heads.
He is our sacrifice, our saviour, why not?
He is sinking and rising into oblivion
at the same time.
He is done measuring for good.

Cubist Newspaper Driven by the Wind

A newspaper, blown and creased by the wind,
wraps itself about a lamppost,
paper columns and rectangular photos,
folds and facets of a Cubist object,
the faces of world leaders crumpled
and kissing the backs of one another's heads,
an explosion and fire at third base,
a line of protesters on a desk in New York,
words collapsing on each other,
phrases cut and clipped into something more poetic
than the daily news, obituaries among the box scores,
suicides in the mutual funds,
a comic dog replaces the word *blaze* in a headline,
words jumbled and fractured in speaking wrinkles
caught in the glare of a lamp,
driven by the wind.

Ball Bearing

The wild river twists and untwists
trying to escape its map.
The mountains hump southward
tired of being photographed.
The fields give in
to the constant *thump thump thump* of boots.
The wind races away from us
and hides high in the trees.
The tall pine holds to its silence
refusing to commune with a creature
whose turbulent mind tumbles
like a ball bearing in its oily sack.

Report on the End of Time

Report on the end of time: it's here, every minute, filling
up with gone tomorrows, yesterday's future. Time
to invest and watch your heart grow, till it
'splodes and showers everybody with five-dollar bills,
to be spent on plastic baubles for the kids, cheap,
real cheap, bottles of wine, a handful of nuts—
almonds or apostrophic cashews. Time ended just
a moment ago, whoops, there it goes again, your
watch is a ribbon tied round the stars, unravelling,
shooting off like a comet in white trailing orgasm,
leaving us behind with the eternal peace
of infinite space—and a bagful of words
our mother packed us to set everything ticking
again.

Blue Sky

Blue sky. No news in it. Light this side.
Light that side, where the sun drones, while
November wrens *cripsh, cripsh* among empty
branches and vines. No nest in the air. Nests
have roots. This isn't the kind of stuff they
talk about on TV. Big empty blue sky. Nothing
noteworthy. No clouds writing. Even the birds
are invisible—their wings so light they too have
dissolved in the brilliance. No journalists. No
cameramen. No hot tips on rising stocks. Just
the blue. Don't adjust your set. Open your
eyes. I toast the blue sky—vast and empty—with
a cup of red tea.

Creation
as
Fresco
Cycle

Villa-Lobos Lugs His Cello Through the Amazon Jungle

Villa-Lobos lugs his cello
through the Amazon jungle.
Where he started out is unimportant.
Where he is headed, untraceable.
No path threads the jungle together,
but when he rests and plays
each leaf takes its perfect place,
the brown-and-green river
bends and bends and never breaks.
Songbirds like shattered stained-glass windows
drawn to the quivering sound,
blink their green eyes
and sharpen their yellow beaks
hoping to compete with the cello's
music in the cool of evening.

At night the musician lays his body
down inside the cello,
feels hollow and trembly
in his vine-draped dreams.
The veins of his wrists like strings.
He dreams an entire orchestra of night
that by morning will be nothing but dew
its music lingering in the triple fan of leaves
in the breathing of umbrella trees.

Thunder

"Deep songs" start in virgin throats,
roses of crimson
outside my second-story window
in the Residencia where Lorca once lived
in old grand Madrid.

Down echoey halls
where the chambermaid sang at two in the afternoon,
his listening once leapt
feasting on birds in the garden of four squares.

He greeted me out of a nap with a single
rolling explosion of thunder rumbling round
my simple scholar's cell.

And now he listens like sunlight to rosebuds
blowing open.

Death of a Poet

In those years the storks of Spain
hatched nightmares of fear
from the innocent skulls
of Guernica's infants,
a black wind rose, its cry
twisted round thin trees
whose dry leaves rattled and ticked.

Lorca's grave is lost
but the words remain.

After the discharge, a lingering silence
carries his song.

Baudelaire's Letter to Ancelle

"I am killing myself—without grief."
I only dress in black now.
My debts do not bother me…
no, no, do not mention my debts.
I am killing myself because I can't live any longer.
I am killing myself because I am a danger to others.
I am killing myself because my logic is lost at sea.
Take care of my negress, Ancelle.
I am killing myself because I believe I am immortal,
because the snow is deep,
because the night is black.
Give her my furniture. Take her as a lover.
Yesterday when we spoke—was I mad?
Of course not.
Tomorrow in a café I will grab a knife
and plant it in my breast.
Will I awake in Hell with a hangover?
Tell my friends I am killing myself
because nothing but claret
is drunk in my mother's house
whereas I prefer burgundy,
because the rain in my heart is falling up,
because Nadar stole my spirit in a photograph.
Between the plunge of the knife
and the final closing of my eyes,
twenty-two years will pass—
the stars will have time to whisper
their bizarre, dark secrets to me,
all the sins they have seen.
I am killing myself
because I am writing a single book of poems,
no more,
but no less.

Double

Was that Baudelaire I saw
tonight trudging through the snow
a curl on his lip
a snarl rising in his throat,
sky a cowl of ink
over a city pure and white?
As usual he was dressed all in black
and questioning, questioning
himself as much as others.
I know how he felt,
this shadow of myself on the snow
dogging me, this shadow
dressed always in black,
this shadow splayed at my feet
by streetlights, this slave,
this black yawning pit
the perfect size, my form's
double, dark mirror.

Creation as Fresco Cycle

The world begins at the upper-left-hand
corner and works across and down.

At first there was nothing but space:
blank, voluptuous, a wall without colour or line.

And pigment: yellow ochre, red earth,
lime-white and black.

Cennini would stipulate, as if describing the sky:
"...put an egg yolk into the blue;
and if the blue is pale,
the yolk should come from a country egg
for they are quite red. Mix it up well."

Fine bristles of miniver fitted into a quill,
a hand appears like a bird in flight.

True fresco: a red line of sinoper
on a layer of *arriccio.*

On the first day, on the second day, et cetera.
"On day six the ox and ass were painted."

Tintoretto

Tintoretto dips his hands in the canals of Venice.
They come out
red
blue
yellow
the hands of the dyer's son
like brushes—
churches and palaces
shimmer on the water.
The ceiling of the sky
churns in chaotic flux:
angels and saints,
flying and falling.
The shimmering paths of Venice reflect
imperfectly
all stable and unstable worlds.
Tintoretto dips his hands in the swirl,
like all good sailors
sent forth by Venice, steadies himself
with the help of the North Star.

Degas in New Orleans

Room crowded with cotton merchants
in black suits,
white shirts,
table of cotton in their midst
glowing like a cloud.
One man reads a newspaper,
black print, white page:
the serious colours of business.

As usual with Degas
we are given an interior view only—
no Mississippi, no musicians on the street,
no black whores calling from balconies—
but the studied ordinary workday
of small-time businessmen.

Objects of white glow with white light
whose source is internal.
No allegory, no message, no meaning.
This is the modern world, as it is,
a frieze of details over a background
of vast boredom, without interpretation.

Boulevard du Temple, Paris, 1839

The early photograph by Daguerre
depicts a gentleman having his boots shined
at a curve in the boulevard.
From our high place we see roofs
of four- and six-story apartments
misting into the distance.
Young trees line the cobbled street and walks
empty of carriages or any other pedestrians save one.
Because he stood still long enough he alone resolved
into history where others moved quickly into dream,
disappearing into their own motions.
The first human recorded in a photograph
leans over a phantom shoe-shiner, hears the clatter
of ghost carriages all round,
horses' hooves shattered into light
where shadows of trees stretch
across the cobbles.
A man with a hat, one leg raised,
stands alone.

Recipe for Light and the Elements

(After viewing an exhibition of the work of Ozias Leduc, Quebec painter)

Cut open an onion, let the light
leak out.
Break open a peach, let spring
ooze forth, rivers run, skies rush.
Halve an apple and release
earth's simple memories.

Inside the melon, a secret
cave of seeds hanging like bats.
Open a lemon and all the clear
charm of desire fills the air.
An orange like a liquid bomb.
The little hairy kiwi, sumptuous flesh.

But an onion—
Place an onion in a dark room
and watch the curious moon
drawn to the window.
The onion burns like a white candle
lit by the knife.

Extracting the Bull
(On viewing 100 Picassos)

Enough complexity.
Give me the bull of a single line
that passes between its horns
and through its heart,
one unbroken thread, sinuous,
holding all the world in, out,
a pulse that rides, a breath,
hardly there at all.
Give me a single line
from past to future
passing through nowhere
a present so fleeting
a bull so alive
it hardly exists at all.

*Love
in
Its
Seasons*

Proud Swimmer
for Faith and Elliot

Handed half an apple
by a pregnant woman
its axis and spine
hung with seeds,
its skin, red night
speckled with stars
and white inside.

On a table across the room
three fuji mums
open as faces of children
falling asleep.

The fetus curls in its brine,
strokes out across black seas,
a tide drawn by the moon,
the smallest of whales flicks its tail,
a phosphorescence rushes to her eyes.

Horses in the Fetal Heart Rate

There in the fetal heart rate
mapped on a graph,
a Muybridge-like repetition
of the furious fetus,
its leaps and dives, its choreography
of horse mountains, its incessant string
of chaos,
virulent line measuring passion.

We see the rocking chair
canter across the front room,
and wind swirling
fallen leaves into a stallion's turn,
while fine lines of text
mirror sleek necks and arcs
of animal grace.

Ragged Edge

At the ragged edge of winter going
that fits to perfection the ragged
edge of spring to come,
my son turning seven
asked of his birth.
He cannot understand how he came
from nothing, will return.
From under the covers he stares at me
in wonder.
        I can only tell him again
how the earth is spinning through space,
give him a home in the universe,
a place to fit ragged answers
to ragged questions.

Male and Female

The one a tower of alphabets and numbers,
the other a body of water
throwing back reflections,
      all the words and figures
      turned backward.

The light keeps drawing veils
across her face.
He too wears a mask
like a metaphor, an equation.

At times he appears to be
a cocoon encrusted with gummy jewels.
She's a red sea
with a deep split in its heart.
The one cannot be touched,
the other, once touched,
never lets go.

There is really only one person
in this room.
All the rest is mental contents.
She creates him.
He creates her.
Everyone is dreaming.
Our imaginations throw shadows
naming it the world.
A hungry bee
grovels inside an oversize flower.
Taxis honk their horns at the display,
the sound of mechanical laughter.

Prisoner

We sat in the kitchen
over the long night's last cup of tea,
smelling the scented Darjeeling steam
(I burned my nose but didn't let on).

A single star waned in the dawn
high in the window it formed
a triangle with us
and using the vision
of Pythagoras
we looked up to measure our closeness.

You wanted to buy my taxi ride home
though I wouldn't allow it
and walked instead,
hands stuffed in pockets,
your long scarf wrapped many times
round my throat.

Heart of Rust

I don't want your heart of stainless steel,
your heart of silver or of gold,
of platinum or diamond,
I want your heart of rust,
rubbed raw and red
by rain, mouldering in the dust,
green sprouts spurting up through every pore,
a heart hot in the sun,
cold in the dark, a heart
for the scrap heap, a heart
for the tenement, the barrio,
the railyard, the factory.

The heart of rust in slow dissolve
like a sunset.

Early Winter Light

I will never tire of this early
winter light
so like your breath
on the pillow asleep
and the streets almost empty
and shining.
There is heat coming
from your face on first waking
still warm with the slow fire
of sleep.
I will never tire of this early
winter light
this light that has no body
of its own
seems like a clear brilliant idea
just a thought on looking up
a thought that joins the sky
at the corner of the desk
two white flowers opening
the only clouds.

Anatomy Lesson

Half a pickle slit lengthwise,
a tadpole tied to the current at one end,
a live wire cut from a stream,
a hot wet wind
blowing through the hole in my head,
a probing stick still attached to a wet bush,
a friendly curious lizard
dressed in slick naugahyde,
a little man, little woman
sliding into her reflection
in a warm throbbing pool,
her tongue in my mouth.

Night Rain in Summer

Beyond the tangle of green vine
lightning bursts open the night sky,
light runs along stems
rain will soon slick.

Hiss of drums on root and leaf
gardens and grasses stretch into emptiness
of steady invisible growth,
greening in silence without pause.

Flowers blossom in the quiet, zucchinis
bloom without a sound, trees rise
another foot each year with no
creak or crack or blast.

Black night, black earth
thunder too has passed,
rain whispers on leaves
everything eases forth with quiet grace.

Nymphalidae

Pater wrote "All the arts aspire to the condition of music." But Mallarme argued that music had to work with relationships which words had already established, and Joyce, though a singer, put himself on the same side. For him all music aspires to the condition of language...

—Richard Ellmann, *Ulysses on the Liffey*

First Snow of Silence

First snow and no birds
sing this morning—
no mourning dove
no trickling sparrows
no gravelly ravens.
Have they been shocked
by the way the world
awoke this morning
lit from below,
as if the white winter sun
emptied itself into the landscape?
I listen and hear no birds,
I who live like an urban hermit
in this city silenced by snow.
Like a mystic anchorite
I long for more snow, more
silence, white acres of it,
streets and yards and houses
muffled under the white mantle.
When silence has reached
a depth as deep as the moon
I will put on Glenn Gould
playing the piano
and watch ice grow in staves
from the eaves.

Tablecloth

In the Montreal restaurant, Le Castillon,
fancy, French, cream-laden,
I notice some unknown seamstress
has taken the trouble
to repair a hole
in the tablecloth
white thread stitched
in ten rows,
      a bit of blank verse
embedded in linen.

A Bird of Three Syllables

How does a word begin?
A bird of three syllables.
Someone throws red leaves in the air
and shouts.
Across the water others who have watched
name things.
Waves whisper in tercets.
Wind combs through the trees
in a language of sighs.
Fecund are the registers of time.
A milch cow, a rabbit, a warren, a hydra.
Through the walls, cadence of neighbours' voices.
A wooden bucket brimmed from a tap
full of watery words.
A gossip slurs a former friend.
Vox caelestis. Vox humana. Vox populi.
Viva voce!

Stars intone deeply somewhere
beyond range of human ear.
Clouds soliloquize grandiloquently.
Say "snow" with passion
and snow appears in the air.

To Quench Our Thirst for Stories

A drafthorse diving into an inkwell...
—Daniel Pennac, *Better Than Life*

A seal slipping out of the black sea
flops about on the white sand beach.
A white swan swims in ink
ducks its slick head under the surface.
A cricket like a hard pellet
scratches black on black.
A crow flaps, flicks ink
from its wings, a black
leopard leaves black stains
on jungle fronds, dissolves
in the grand piano.
The penguins, like Paris surrealists,
wear bow ties
painted on with India ink.
At the water hole thick and black
the lion rips free the windpipe of an addax,
both stand in ink to their heaving chests.
In the swamp, the beaver slick with ink,
in the dirt, the ant, a pure black drop,
across the sky a dragon
spits black flags of ink in the wind:
the silence of ink is deadly
when it speaks and no one listens.

Cigar Box

Faintest wisp of cigar-box cedar,
the brand-new book from Andre Deutsch.
Each new volume holds its own smell,
each publisher its signature odour.
Slight, palest yellow memories of spruce,
pine, fir, light falling in clouds
among branches, in pools on the ground.
And ink, redolent of damp earth and night,
deep with meaning, grass and moss.
Smell is our most primitive sense,
poems enter the nostrils first and flare,
leave a smoking trail of words.

On Reading Submissions to a Poetry Magazine

Dangerous confidences,
poets so cavalier
with their privates, their dreams,
drugged, quotidian, shamelessly
alike each other's,
abusing the same
five hundred words.

Give me a page that ignites
in the hands, sounds
with vision, slap of the sea
in the reader's face—be fearless!
Horses of Arctic wind, poems
so spare and flashing
we realize we have been starved
for them, words
bright as iridium
or lush and cinnamon-scented
if lush is what
they long to be.

I want to know no one's secrets—
I've my own, the same.
Deep draughts of St-Julien Bordeaux,
a week without eating
laid out on a granite slab,
sunlight burning a hole
through your dictionary,
a rhyme for Betelgeuse,
a stub of cigar smoking still
on the concrete—
What did the smoker look like?
Find him. Listen
to his voice, the river of gravel

smoking from his throat.
Feast on the world. Be kind
with words.

Crackle-Glaze

Listening to birds at dusk,
my heart all ears,
crackle-glaze clouds break up
under puzzle pieces of blue sky.
But the birds, a chorus
as in a Greek play
that comes to its end each evening,
my heart a great throbbing ear
pulses as it listens.
I heard the same birds at dawn,
singing their opening lines,
when the sky was young,
clouds moist with life.

The Space Between Two Words

A page from Leonardo's Leicester Codex
shimmers under a half inch of water,
a mirage of bent light on a map.

Where is that place?
The space between two words.
What two words?
It matters not.
What matters is the space
the silence held
just long enough
so that everyone looks up,
wondering, Will he go on?
And he does.

But where is that place,
the one written in Arabic
on the map
shimmering underwater?

I will take you there, he says.
They both fall silent
and sip their tea,
knowing they will never go.

Listening

The lake listens to the high noonday sun.
The mirror listens to your face growing old.
Leaves listen to wind and shiver with finesse.
The darkness listens to the crickets
who complain incessantly and roll over in their sleep.
Backyards listen to a few lingering stars.
Paper listens to time and turns yellow,
curls at the edge, is forgotten and remembered.
Swallows listen to air while watermelons
listen to deep swollen silences out of the earth.
Sleepers listen to dreams of waking.
Bees listen to the call and cry of flowers,
flies listen to fields of manure in ravishing repose.
Words listen for punctuation, then change direction,
soldiers marching across a parade ground.
I listen to my neighbour crash into his pool
in darkness at night into black waters.
Silence listening in silence.

Old
Bones
Juggles
Three
Skulls

When You Will Be a Mountain

When you will be a mountain
will you write with your streams
all down the valley?
When you will be the sky
will you write with the flights of birds
soaring to horizons?
When you will be night
will you write the way
stars appear at dusk,
gathering, gathering, until all is said,
until silence is shaped and soothed?

Skull

My nose has left its face
because it seeks the impossible perfect
vial of perfume,
it longs to perch on the bottle's lip
and dream in
lush jets of scent.
My ears abandon their head
seeking a music I cannot contrive,
inside a piano, inside a cornet
inside a drum a trombone a violin.
My tongue left long ago—
it wants to taste the words
it speaks
in a kind of self-communion,
a redemption of wasted words and more:
language itself.
Eyes too wander away,
desirous of visions
lit violet.

Left empty, the skull
hums a sad tune
with the help of the wind.

Lombardy Poplars

In the distance
there are always Lombardy poplars,
whether in memory, story, or film,
the characters drive lazily down
the Appian Way
or parade somberly
along a street in a small Quebec town,
a funeral for a shopkeeper,
or lovers stroll on the outskirts
of Buenos Aires,
hardly aware of the trees,
the frieze of Lombardy poplars,
so tall, striking into the light
the lovers cannot help but notice
and feel slightly dizzy at their height,
and yet, the Lombardy poplars
hardly sway at all
in the quiet afternoon breeze
just sink their roots deeper,
deeper into dark.

Old Bones

Old bones juggles three skulls,
one still wears spectacles—
perhaps he'd like something to read?
Death in Venice or the *Tibetan Book of the Dead.*
Time ticks by, there's no foothold,
no handhold in these passing clouds.
The candle burns down, its flame
erasing nights, crickets twittering,
distant traffic drones on.

I take a drink of water,
my wife reads a book by lamplight.
Outside the cabin, small bats
stitch back and forth,
netting us in ropes of dark air.

Once a Great Ruler, This Spider

Once a great ruler, this spider has come
to visit me, late at night, to speak
of death, and the great wind of time
and history.
                    Death is small, he says, no more
than a trinket at the throat of a woman
where the pulse is seen, throbbing
from shadow to light.
                    The wind of time, he says,
twists in ever-tightening circles, picks up the dust,
lays it down, brings rain and takes rain
away.
          He is far from the jungle, this spider,
so he spins a jungle out of words.

No One Will Be Counting

One day sunlight
will pass through my empty eye sockets
and light up the back of my skull.
The chill mountain stream will flow up
my pelvis and out my mouth.
Grey and gold finches twittering in nearby bushes
will not be frightened by my presence.
Later, the dark will attract a curious moon
but no one will be counting.
These words will be long-forgotten.

Tonight while snow flies outside my window,
green grapes taste sweet.

Albert

Albert,
gone a year, I reread
your letters and note the several
times you mention suicide,
your easy way with words
and all the women you went through.
I picture you sitting on the drill rig
off Newfoundland, Bartók's waves
washing through your Walkman,
reading back issues of *Atlantic*
and *Saturday Night*, three weeks on,
three weeks off to drink and drug,
out in the North Atlantic
working the night shift
tracking icebergs.
We wrote often in those years
you including haiku, your comments
on poems I had sent,
then the letters trailed off
near the end
as if you wanted to drift away.
But I remember when you came
to Ottawa on your yearly jaunt
to escape Newfoundland's mizzle
and the inbred social life
of St. John's, I was teaching
a poetry class at a local high school
and invited you to speak on haiku
and you did, in your high-strung way,
eyes almost invisible behind thick glasses,
tall and thin and gesticulating about
how haiku are "found, found,
not imagined" and talking on and on
(obsessively as you always did)

to fifty students in the auditorium,
hard-edged high-schoolers amazed
as you backed, talking, into a pile
of metal folding chairs stacked
against the wall, falling backward
into them with a calamitous racket,
talking, talking, and never once missing
the beat or losing your train of thought.
There was a haiku there.

You had a mind
so strong and hard it did you more
harm than good.
Brilliant at chemistry, philosophy, literature,
you even took up pottery and made rough
beautiful raku until your wife left,
and then you turned to photography
telling me how you spent weeks
working on a single photograph
of a gull piercing the sky
until there was nothing left
but a slight calligraphy of light
and then that too disappeared.

Once, a few months ago you came
in a dream and said you hadn't
died but had only gone travelling
alone to the Far North
but I awoke
and you didn't.

The last time you visited
you spoke about driving,
just setting out driving at night
with no destination
as we used to do in the old days

up around Lake Superior from Toronto
driving on adrenaline and talk talk talk
until late silence came down
and only the stare of northern stars remained
and the steady thrum of the engine
and those two headlights searching
for we knew not what.
We drove until the driving and the talk
were burned out of us
and then we limped back home.

Owl-like, huge ears, weak eyes,
night was your time.
You would sit at my kitchen table
drinking saki or Chianti
or rum you had brought from the island
listening to what I had written
or something I had read
and then you'd iron your best pants
and head out into the night
to visit the bars, first in Ottawa
then over into Hull for the late frenzy
not necessarily on the hunt
but looking for the energy,
nursing two or three beers all evening
then tiptoeing into the house at 4:00 a.m.
not wanting to wake the wife or child.

Your saving grace was a sense of humour.
It must have abandoned you at the end,
or maybe not.
For all your reading in Zen I don't know
if you practised much
although a friend said
you were found, after the poison,
sitting in meditation.

Death leaves all these unanswerable ambiguities
and a pile of letters
and the cheque you left
last time you were here
for long-distance phone calls you made.
A blank cheque made out to me
signed by you
never cashed.

Wilderness

Creation Myths

Wind blew dust in the water.

Old Crow counted the stars, added them up.

The moon fell to earth and split
open like a fruit, spilling seeds.

Old Crow sneezed and stars came flying out
                    both his ears.

A flower split a stone.
The earth went spinning in two directions.

Old Crow tried counting backward from a million.
A blue jay screamed
and the whole forest listened.

Old Crow left in search
of the four corners of space,
found his footprints
before he made them.

Music in the air
had not yet entered the flute.

Old Crow laughed and fire
leapt from dry wood.

Snow started falling as we entered the dream.

Old Crow noticed the black soil smelled like violets.

Slowly, slowly, the shadow of a fern
crept away from the first rising sun.

A comet got caught in Old Crow's feathers,
spinning him in circles.

A bluebird fell in a pool of sky pigment.
Snow filled up the morning glory.

Nine Haiku

Day after day
suns pile up like melons
over the western hills.

Setting them down together
on the couch, the cordless
telephone wears eyeglasses.

The library lights flash
off and on at closing time,
I'm reading about fireflies.

A morning so cold
even the teenagers
wear hats.

First day of spring,
I welcome the fly
to my house.

A cold day in spring,
in a yard on a block of ice
a tattered telephone book.

Collapsible umbrella
upside down on a hanger,
a bat in its sleep.

Reading about deep ecology,
I see an old mother walk by
under a green umbrella.

Handwritten sign
along a country road:
FIREWORKS AND STRAWBERRIES.

Reinventing the World

Napoleon's soldiers are marching
backward out of Russia,
the deconstruction of the great cities
New York, Chicago, São Paulo
begins without a moment's hesitation—
every rivet, every bolt and pane of glass
disassembled, it is the end of the world
coming quite gently as it must.
It is time for bullets to leap back
into the rifles of soldiers,
time for aggression to turn
seeking its source within the cloudy brain,
travelling inward, time for ships
to back up across the seas,
time for Magellan to unwind the world,
time to leave the Pacific to itself,
its quiet ways, who knows what it did
before we began looking, it is time
for peoples to forget all languages,
wind down from Babel, taking stone
from stone under a sky of silence,
time for the wind to return all the sand
into mountains, time to reassemble
ancient statues in the fields,
time to unplough the furrow, to heal
that wound, to forget all that was
and seems to be, time to wander
backward through the night from dawn
to dusk, releasing the animals
back to the wild, freeing the cities
from their walls, fish to eggs,
bird back into assembling shell,
sea into the mouth of God,
stars into the void.

Wall

The wall hides something but has its own face.
Behind the wall glittering with mosaics
lurks the worst slum she has ever seen.
Another wall is ancient, scarred, weathered,
the earth made to stand up like man
revealing its face of faults and scarps,
its cracks of road and dried-up riverbed,
its anticlines and synclines.
A wall bathed in light quickens in me
the scent of lemons
drifting through the village at evening.
A white wall is a simple death.
Wailing wall is writhing with words
crammed in every crevice,
petitions to the god of walls.
The wall keeps you in, keeps you out.
Like the face of a stranger you pass on the street,
it has no window.
The wall is a waterfall of stone
pouring in a sheet from the roof.
Out of the wall leap films of buffalo
and toucans and moose and Berbers on camels,
and when the film is shut off
they go back into the wall.
The wall has nicks from bullets
that passed through democrats, priests, deposed tyrants.
The wall has a fountain mounted on it,
a mouth from which water pours into a basin,
overflowing into a Roman street.
The wall is full of hooks or dials or electronic boards.
The Great Wall keeps China protected
from barbarians to the north.
Through a hole in a Greek wall,
the Aegean Sea shines blue.

On another, a fresco depicts a naked couple romping.
The bedroom wall holds a copy of Matisse's jazz dancer.
The beige wall's expanse is broken by a single electric
outlet one foot from the floor.
The walls of Jericho, the walls of the Alamo,
the walls of Fortress Quebec, the walls of Chirico
and Magritte, the wall behind the Last Supper.
The wall is not a clock but a calendar.
A lone wall stands in the desert, in the Arctic,
in an orchard.
The wall has lost all meaning, ghosts pass through it.

Wilderness

No maps.
No street signs.
No scouts. No trail blazers. No trackers.
No tracks to track.
No one has passed this way before.
No conductor calling out the stops.
No names. No new names. No familiars.
Nothing known or described.
Nothing plotted on graph paper. No grids that fit.
No echo. No reason.
No tracings in the dust.
No punctuation. No timed pauses.
No directions. No sextant.
No configurations of planets. No prophetic dreams.
No voice whispering.
No lights to follow, on land or sea.
No horse to ride that knows its way home.
No instructions. No command.
No suggestions. No referrals.
No compass. No rudders. No path.
No scent to follow.
Nothing shining in the distance.
No sense of one foot following another.
Nowhere to get to.
No one keeping count.
No one measuring the distance.
No secret message. No invisible ink.
No pattern. No order. No chaos.
No narrow path to high mountains.
No wide path across prairies.
No end. Nowhere to begin.

Mᴀʀᴋ Fʀᴜᴛᴋɪɴ has published two previous volumes of poetry, *Acts of Light* and *The Alchemy of Clouds*. The Governor General's Award nominee has also published six novels, including *Slow Lightning*, *The Lion of Venice*, *Atmospheres Apollinaire*, and *Invading Tibet*. His work has appeared in the United States, England, Holland, and India, as well as Canada. He lives in Ottawa, Ontario.